MEDIA F⦾CUS

Popular Music

Roger Thomas

First published in Great Britain by Heinemann Library
Halley Court, Jordan Hill, Oxford OX2 8EJ
a division of Reed Educational and Professional Publishing Ltd.
Heinemann is a registered trademark of Reed Educational & Professional Publishing Ltd.

OXFORD MELBOURNE AUCKLAND
JOHANNESBURG BLANTYRE GABORONE
IBADAN PORTSMOUTH (NH) USA CHICAGO

Designed by Visual Image
Printed in Hong Kong

03 02 01 00
10 9 8 7 6 5 4 3 2

ISBN 0 431 08212 X

British Library Cataloguing in Publication Data
Thomas, Roger
    Popular music. – (Media focus)
    1. Music trade – Juvenile literature 2. Popular music – Juvenile literature
    I. Title
    338.4'7'782'421766

Acknowledgements
The Publishers would like to thank the following for permission to reproduce photographs:
All Action/Doug Peters, p. 25; BPI, p. 5; Brand New Products, p. 12; E Map Metro (*Kerrang, Mixmag, Q*), p. 24; EMI Classics, p. 4; Kobal Collection, pp. 22t 231, /Darren Michaels 23r; London Features International Ltd, pp. 8/Sam Hain, 9, 20, 29; Mercury Records Ltd, p. 7; *New Musical Express*/IPC, p. 24; Polygram Video Ltd/Alex Bailey, p. 22b; Redferns/Leon Moris p. 14, /Mick Hutson, p. 11; Rex Features/Frazer, p. 13; *Rhythm*/Future Publishing, p. 24; Select Music & Video Distribution, p. 6; Sony Images p. 18; SSEYO Ltd, p. 26; Virgin Records Ltd, p.15. Commissioned photographs by Chris Honeywell.

The publishers would like to thank the following for permission to reproduce copyright material:
P 17, 'Radio Ga Ga', Words and music by Roger Taylor. © 1983 Queen Music Ltd, EMI Music Publishing Ltd, London WC2H 0EA. Reproduced by permission of IMP Ltd. 'No Particular Place to Go' by Chuck Berry © 1964 Arc Music Corp. By kind permission of Jewel Music Publishing Company Ltd.

Cover photograph reproduced with permission of Tony Stone Images (Lester Lejkowitz).

Our thanks to Steve Beckingham, Head of Media Studies, Fakenham College, Norfolk for his comments in the preparation of this book.

Every effort has been made to contact copyright holders of any material reproduced in this book. Any omissions will be rectified in subsequent printings if notice is given to the Publisher.

Any words appearing in the text in bold, **like this**, are explained in the Glossary.

Contents

Introduction

When popular music became recognized as a separate form of music, many people expected it to be a passing fad. However, the music business is now worth £2.5 billion a year to the UK economy, of which £1.25 billion is revenue from overseas. The industry employs 115,000 people in the UK alone.

As a media phenomenon, popular music began in live performance, then incorporated printed music, then came to dominate the broadcasting and record industries. Since then, popular music has become one of the most powerful artistic and commercial forces in the world. This book is about the complex relationships that exist between popular music and the media.

How did popular music begin?

In the original sense of the word, 'popular' music is nothing of the sort!

Music is probably as old as the human race, but the idea of 'popular music' is surprisingly recent. Until the eighteenth century, European music was traditionally divided into:
• 'art music' – composed and performed in towns and cities for the benefit of educated, wealthy people
• 'folk music' – sung and played by working people while they worked, rested or celebrated.

The earliest forms of popular music were halfway between the two. In ancient times professional musicians and dancers would move from town to town, entertaining the residents with songs and shows that mixed the informal themes of folk music with the more formal presentation of art music. During the Middle Ages, musicians and singers called 'troubadours' and 'minstrels' would travel throughout Europe, performing in the same way.

The most important difference between this early popular music and folk music was that folk music had always been an unpaid, informal, social activity. Early folk music was often performed by amateur singers and musicians who would have had work to do as well. Many people would often join in, singing or dancing if they did not play an instrument, meaning that the performers were also the audience. This tradition survives today in, for example, pub songs and holiday sing-alongs. This differed from early popular music which

The Beggar's Opera

This recording of The Beggar's Opera *dates from the late 1950s.*

Quite apart from the music it contained, *The Beggar's Opera* had many other similarities with contemporary popular music.
• It affected musical fashions. After the first performance, Italian opera was out and ballad opera was in – at least for a while!
• It toured widely. As well as being performed in London, the show was taken to other major cities.
• It used **merchandising**. While the T-shirt had yet to be invented, it was possible to buy accessories and ornaments which had the words of the show's most popular songs on them.
• It created megastars with their own fanclubs and magazines. Lavinia Fenton, who played the lead female role, became a cult celebrity. Her biography was written and circulated, poetry was dedicated to her, and pamphlets of her sayings and jokes were produced.

was performed for an audience who would pay the performer.

The same distinction really still exists today. Interestingly, dictionaries define 'popular' as meaning 'of, or carried on by, the people', which is a description more suited to folk music. Perhaps a more accurate name would have been 'populist music', meaning a music created by an élite for consumption by a popular audience. The idea of 'popular music' as 'music which appeals to the largest available audience when compared to other forms of music' is perhaps the most useful definition.

High art for all?

The Beggar's Opera was first performed in 1728 and marks one of the most important points in the early history of popular music. Written by John Gay, an English poet and playwright, it combined the art music tradition of Italian opera with the folk music tradition of ballads and rather rude songs to produce an immensely popular entertainment which audiences still enjoy today. *The Beggar's Opera*

First stop for facts

The British Phonographic Industry (BPI) is one of the most important organizations in popular music. It represents the interests of the record industry at the highest levels.

The BPI is also the definitive source for up-to-date and comparative sales figures, awards received and revenue made by different kinds of music and different kinds of recorded formats. Most of the figures mentioned in this book are taken from BPI information.

Don't be sure of anything until you've checked with the latest from the BPI!

is perhaps the earliest recognizable ancestor of modern popular music.

Publishing and recording

As the tradition of music as popular entertainment continued to grow, popular songs were gathered into collections and published as sheet music.

Recorded sound

By the 1890s, the music publishing industry had become firmly established. Sound recordings, however, were being made on wax cylinders, which were very expensive, as they had to be cut individually. In the early twentieth century, it became possible to mass-produce shellac records, which could be stamped out quickly and in vast numbers on factory machinery. This process of mass-producing copies of recorded music was eventually to become the most important part of the popular music industry.

DID YOU KNOW?•FACTS & FIGURES•INDUSTRY RESEARCH•INDUSTRY STATISTICS•VITAL STATISTICS•

The BPI on the net

BPI

THE BPI MAINTAINS AN EXCELLENT SITE ON THE INTERNET, AT WWW.BPI.CO.UK, WHERE ALL THE LATEST FIGURES ARE AVAILABLE, TOGETHER WITH HELPFUL COMMENTS ON WHAT THEY MEAN. THE SITE ALSO GIVES DETAILS OF THE BPI'S MANY PUBLICATIONS, INCLUDING A HANDBOOK OF STATISTICS, A GUIDE TO CAREERS IN THE MUSIC BUSINESS, A GUIDE TO MUSIC COURSES AND BOOKS ABOUT HOW MUCH THE INDUSTRY IS WORTH, BOTH AT HOME AND IN THE EXPORT MARKET.

What is popular music today?

And with whom is it popular anyway?

Many attempts have been made to define popular music, but perhaps because we are surrounded by it, and because it reaches us in so many different ways, it has always been hard to come up with an objective and precise definition. However, there are some attributes that popular music has always had, and which still hold true for modern pop music.

Many people make a simple distinction between classical and popular music. By

Spotter's guide to pop

Pop music is usually:

• short – the traditional length for a pop song being around three minutes
• simple and melodic
• either lively and rhythmic or slow and thoughtful – but rarely both in the same song!
• written with **lyrics** (words) that deal with ideas or images easily identified by a wide audience – emotional states, relationships, or social activities such as dancing or partying are frequent themes.

Although these definitions are important to the style of the music, it is also true that the aim of successful pop music is to sell as many recordings and concert tickets as possible. This contrasts with, for example, classical music or jazz, which are aimed at more specialist markets, with no anticipation of large-scale commercial success among non-specialist listeners.

'classical' music they usually mean the European tradition of composition and performance which began in the Christian church in the Middle Ages. This music began as Christian devotional music for voices only. Instruments were associated with folk music, which was considered crude and noisy and therefore offensive to God.

Later, instruments became acceptable. Patronage of the music then passed to the aristocracy and the Royal Courts, and eventually to specialist music colleges, sometimes known as conservatories. Many British music colleges retain their courtly connections in their names, such as the Royal College of Music and the Royal Scottish Academy of Music and Drama. This 'classical' tradition includes composers such as Bach, Beethoven and Mozart and is still supported today, with living composers continuing to write music for classical orchestras, choirs, groups and soloists, and with many young musicians learning how to play classical music. Many people would still rather listen to this music than any other kind, and they tend to think of popular music as being any music that is not classical. They also tend to think that classical music contains more complex ideas than popular music.

The problem with this definition is that there are many pieces of classical music that are in the real sense very popular, or have been made so through marketing, often in association with some non-musical concept. In musical terms, these examples of 'popular classical' music will often have what classical musicians call 'big tunes' – clear main melodies which are as easy to recognize and listen to as the most ordinary of pop songs. On the other hand, there are many examples of so-called 'popular' music that use many of the traditions of the pop song but which are not at all popular in any real sense.

Influences

Today, virtually any influence can be found within popular music. The wide availability of music through recording and broadcasting has meant that musicians and listeners have been able to discover an enormous range of musical styles and to listen to older styles of popular music preserved by recordings. All these types of music are constantly being discovered, rediscovered and mixed together to create new musical styles.

One example is world music, a rather Eurocentric term for the music of non-European cultures, which have been a rich source of ideas for popular music.

Popular classics?

This compilation below is a good example of how classical music can be offered to listeners who would traditionally be associated with the pop market. The CD was released during the 1998 World Cup and was sold in the classical departments of record shops. The music is approachable and recognizable. The concept also makes use of the enthusiasm for music traditionally associated with football, from terrace chants to football singles. Also, the Naxos label specializes in producing very low-priced classical recordings – currently £4.99 per single disc in the UK – making it an inexpensive impulse purchase or gift for a football fan. The music itself, however, is mostly 'straight' classical music.

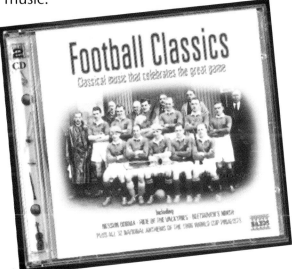

Unpopular pop?

By contrast, Scott Walker's *Tilt* CD appears at first glance to be 'popular' music. The artist has had a long career in the pop world, firstly as a member of The Walker Brothers, noted for their yearning, emotional pop songs, and later as a soloist.

However, *Tilt* is a profound and uncompromising work, with haunting, surreal lyrics and complex, demanding musical ideas quite unlike any form of rock or pop music.

Who makes popular music?

During this century, popular music has been reinvented many times. But how?

Popular music has always relied heavily on style. This can be in many forms:

Compositional style

Within the various types of popular music, any innovative musical ideas that can be added to a composition will often help to draw attention to it. For example, the 1997 single 'C'est La Vie' by the group B*Witched contained a short section of Irish folk dance music, which was very distinctive. It capitalized on the fact that the group come from Ireland and also on the popularity of Irish music caused by the hugely successful Irish dance stage show *Riverdance*.

Instrumental style

Despite – or perhaps because of – the fact that modern pop production techniques will tend to disguise the contributions made by individual musicians, unusual instrumental resources and approaches remain important, and genuine instrumental innovations always stand out. For example, Radiohead's 'No Surprises' on their best-selling album *OK Computer* features a sad, gentle recurring melody played on a glockenspiel, which is hardly a traditional pop/rock instrument.

Vocal style

Most mainstream popular music uses the song form, and an easily recognizable lead voice often makes the difference between the success or failure of the song, both artistically and commercially. For example, the use of regional accents by singers is often distinctive, and often faked – the Beatles were once asked

B*Witched were able to show off their 'Irishness' on the video for C'est la vie, by including a short section of Irish dancing.

why they sang like Americans! On the other hand, Cerys Richards, lead singer with Catatonia, has a Welsh accent which helps to make the band's songs immediately recognizable and unique. If you know Catatonia's song 'Road Rage', try to imagine it being sung by Boy George!

Presentational style

This is crucial both on stage and through the medium of recordings. Attitude, body language, stage set design, album cover design and dress style can combine to convey an image that suits the music. This can convey aggression (Prodigy), sexuality (Madonna), mystery (Portishead) or any other impression, such as humour, humility or even despair, which will help to make the overall presentation of the performers and their music distinctive.

From listener to performer

One interesting characteristic of popular music during this century is the way in which the performers and the audience seem to keep changing places!

Popular music is of course exactly that – popular – and ever since the genre began, most performers have begun their musical lives as listeners to the music. This contrasts with, for example, Western classical music, where beginners – usually children – learn simple tunes and musical exercises which introduce them to the beginnings of classical technique, but they may well have little or no experience of listening to the 'real' classical music which they will eventually learn to play.

Two examples of this process at work:
• drummer Dylan Howe, son of legendary rock guitarist Steve Howe, grew up in a household surrounded by rock music and rock instruments and was attracted to the drumkit in his father's home studio at the age of 11: 'I saw it shining there and I started to hit it!'
• DJ Mrs Wood spent her early career working for various record companies, developing an interest in DJ-ing as a result of hearing dance records brought in by the artists.

Having realized that they are able to express themselves through music, some artists will feel moved to convey a message to their audiences as well as entertain them, and they are often very effective. The message may be political (singer/songwriter Billy Bragg), humanitarian (Sting's 'They Dance Alone', a song about human rights in Chile) or personal (Tori Amos has drawn on her experience of kidnap and rape).

It is significant that, in all the above cases, the artistic impulse came first and the need to convey a message second. When the process is reversed, things can often backfire. The English contemporary classical composer Cornelius Cardew (1936–81) held strong left-wing views. Reasoning that his music was too academic to appeal to working people he opted instead to write simple music and songs, which were much closer to popular music in style. Unfortunately, although these songs were performed by his group at political rallies, they had little impact on their target audience.

Keith Flint of Prodigy is often described as an aggressive performer. However, such images are usually used in a knowing, comic-strip way – a conspiracy of irony shared with the audience but which excludes those who make the mistake of taking it seriously – such as the audience's parents!

Who makes music popular?

Much of the talent, risk and sheer hard work involved in producing popular music is completely hidden from the public.

The production of popular music today is a long, complex process involving the different skills and abilities of a great number of people. This was not always the case. For example, medieval troubadours would often write and perform their own songs, or reinterpret traditional songs, play them to audiences and collect their payment. In the days when sheet music ruled supreme, things were only slightly more complicated. The songwriter would simply need to have his or her work accepted by a publisher, who would then produce and sell the music and pay the songwriter.

However, with the invention of sound recording, the performer became the most important element in this process. As travel, communications and audience expectations became more and more sophisticated, the ability, style, image and presentation of the performer became predominant — what now mattered was the end product. People became less interested in listening out for attractive songs and tunes that could theoretically be included in any artist's repertoire. Instead, their attention would focus first of all on the skills of the artist. While the demand for quality songwriting and musical skills remained, these talents — and the people who had these talents — effectively became 'hidden' behind the public face of the performer.

Today there is a long chain of activity which has to be set in motion in order to produce a piece of popular music, often involving all of the people listed on the opposite page.

Music, the media, motivation and credibility

Many performers present their work in the field of popular music as a contribution to music as an art form. They are often disapproving of other artists who appear to place commercial success before artistic effort, and even express this in their **lyrics**.

• In his song 'Tinseltown Rebellion', the American composer and performer Frank Zappa showed his contempt for capable musicians from comfortable, middle-class backgrounds who pretended to be rebellious and aggressive in order to achieve commercial success.

• The British band James attacked heavily-hyped 'personality' bands in their song 'Destiny Calling'.

• Over 25 years ago, the American musician and humorist Martin Mull performed a mock blues song which satirised rich and successful blues singers who still sang about oppression and poverty. In the song, the bluesman wakes up in the afternoon (not 'this morning'!) to discover both his cars have been stolen; he is so distressed he throws his drink across the lawn.

• The British humorous songwriter Neil Innes wrote a song condemning the poor musical standards and juvenile lyrics of the material used in the Eurovision Song Contest. The song was called 'Bing Bang Bong'!

The artist/s

People choose to become popular musicians for many reasons. Often the most simple of these is the self-discovery of some form of musical skill combined with the motivation to put this into practice in the context of popular music, initially at an amateur or semi-professional level. The motivation can be equally simple – someone may just love performing music, or be attracted to the music's social lifestyle. It can also, however, be quite complex:

• singer and songwriter Jon Anderson has said that there were only two ways to escape from his rural background – becoming a successful footballer, or becoming a pop star

• songwriter and musician John Cale found himself rebelling against his rather staid training in classical music by becoming a rock musician and producer

• moving from another high-profile profession into pop music is often a good career move, such as in the cases of Samantha Fox (model), Kylie Minogue (actress), and David Baddiel and Frank Skinner (comedians).

The manager

Most bands and soloists with substantial careers will need to employ a manager to handle their business affairs, including liaising with concert promoters and record companies. Managers may also deal with press and publicity or, if their artists have a sufficiently high profile, they will hand these tasks over to a publicist and possibly a record company plugger, a type of publicist who specializes in getting records broadcast on radio and television.

The concert promoter

These range from large companies who organize massive events, to individuals who arrange gigs in their local pub – but the problems are essentially the same: ensuring there's an audience, hoping the performers will be on form, dealing with ticketing, publicity, security and so on. Many concerts – even big events with tickets costing upwards of £30 – can lose money. Occasionally, this is allowed for in advance, as tours are often used more as a means of promoting a new record than as money-making events in themselves.

The record industry

This is the central pillar of the modern popular music industry. In the eyes and ears of the audience, recordings are the most 'public' aspect of popular music. Despite music being a live art form, many people actually experience popular music mostly through recordings.

James: a band with strong views about hype.

11

Live!

While the distinction between live and recorded music is becoming increasingly blurred, the process of putting on a live event remains as complicated as ever.

In the early days of modern pop music in the late fifties and early sixties, live performance was a relatively simple affair. At its best, a concert would involve a band who were competent performers, with instruments of reasonable quality and **amplification** that would at least carry the sound throughout the venue.

However, there were many opportunities for problems to arise. Audience expectations were often low, and musicians would often perform in public before they had reached a reasonable standard of musicianship. Factors such as a trade embargo with America meant that quality instruments were not widely available in the UK, so performers would often use poorly crafted instruments from Russia or Eastern Europe. Venues were mainly geared to dance bands or traditional jazz and rarely had adequate **PA** facilities or lighting. Electrical equipment would often malfunction.

Live or recorded?

Recording technology and production techniques are always improving, enabling musicians to release records of a very high quality – higher, in fact, than is easily achievable in a live performance. Yet audiences expect the same standards in live performance as offered by recordings, which puts the artists, sound engineers and producers under immense pressure.

For example:
• Many performances on television are wholly or partly mimed by the performers to avoid the unpredictability of a live set.
• Look out for electric guitars and keyboards which aren't connected to amplifiers and therefore can't possibly be making any sound!
• Drummers can buy noiseless 'playback cymbals' for miming on video and TV appearances.

These look like cymbals and move like real ones – but they make no sound other than a muffled click. They are plastic 'playback cymbals', designed for miming!

• Often a particular sound or effect that works very well on record is impossible to duplicate live. One example is double-tracking the lead singer's voice, which is clearly impossible in real life.

Rising standards

Today, the higher standard of musicianship in popular music, the much-improved quality of instruments and equipment, and the availability of either purpose-built, or at least suitably refurbished, venues have caused standards to rise considerably.

Rising expectations

However, audience expectations are also now far higher. This is partly because several generations have now grown up with popular music, both as players and listeners, and have sufficient experience of the music to evaluate its quality. The other important factor has been the high standard of recording which is now possible, adding to the artists' talents using **editing** and **overdubbing** techniques, together with additional **session musicians** when necessary, to produce a perfectly crafted end result.

An enormous amount of work goes into staging a performance of popular music, particularly a large event like this Live Aid concert.

Recreating the record

Making concerts sound as good as records is not always easy and will occasionally demand that recorded or **sequenced** backing tracks are mixed into the live sound. There have been occasions when the problem has proved so insurmountable that entire performances have to be mimed to recorded backing. This has been known to go wrong, with disastrous results.

How a concert happens

Before a concert:
• the artists rehearse a set of material until they are satisfied with their performance. Many factors influence the content of their show. Have they got a new album to promote? If so, this material will be heavily featured. Are they playing to a new audience (say, on their first international tour), who need to be impressed, or to supportive fans, who want to hear their favourite songs? Is there some material that is less effective live than on record?
• the promoter reaches an agreement for payment with the artists and venue, sets ticket prices, arranges the sales of tickets through agents, invites the media and liaises with …
• the venue management, who is either promoting the event themselves, or who has hired their venue out to an external promoter. The venue management also provides the promotor with a range of services – selling tickets, publicity, **merchandising**, and so on.

Recording and the media

Recorded music and the media that serve this industry depend on each other in many ways – some obvious, some very subtle.

Why make records?

Mostly, a recording is a fairly straightforward attempt by a record company to make money through a popular art form – which is reasonable enough. On the other hand, artists will often make recordings which they fund themselves. Such recordings may be made for purely artistic reasons. They may also serve to further the career of the performers by attracting publicity. Also in many specialist categories such as dance music, which is often recorded inexpensively with electronic instruments, an independent recording can be supplied directly to a specialist market and provide a reasonable profit for the musicians and producer.

Commercially viable recordings can be made using cheap equipment which people can set up at home.

From A&R to HMV

For commercial record companies, the procedure for releasing records begins with the A&R (Artists and Repertoire) person, who is usually a full-time employee of an individual record company, and whose job it is to identify performers who could be successful recording artists.

The decision to offer a record deal to an artist will depend on whether the music is of a marketable standard and suited to market trends, but this need not mean slavishly following fashion, as an imaginative and different approach will often succeed if it contrasts interestingly with the music around it, such as the first album by Gomez. This is, however, very much a part of the financial and artistic risks associated with the record business.

A&R people spend much of their working lives going to performances by new bands and listening to tapes which bands send in to record companies in the hope of attracting a record deal. This sounds fun, but it can be very hard work. An A&R person may find themselves travelling from one end of the country to the other to hear a band or artist who turns out to be dreadful.

The A&R departments of record companies are constantly receiving tapes from budding pop stars, and A&R staff often have to make very rapid decisions as to which new artists are worth investigating further. It's therefore important that the opening minute of the first

Gomez

Gomez are a band who present an innovative combination of image and music. Their musical style is derived from a gruff, deadpan interpretation of American country blues, mixed with inventive arrangements and unexpected melodic ideas. This contrasts with their onstage image, as the band are not only English, but also young and quite ordinary in appearance.

song on a new band's tape is very good indeed, because that's often all that gets listened to!

Once an artist or band has been signed to a record company, the business of making records gets under way. This requires the services of a record producer, who will guide the artists' creativity through the processes of recording (assisted by a recording engineer).

Once the music exists in a listenable recorded form as a 'master' (the final, artistically and technically complete version from which the

records will be copied) the remaining stages in the process can get underway. These include:

- design for the CD cover and any related advertising
- advertising, marketing and promotion, using the press and broadcast media
- manufacturing the CD – a process that has become increasingly inexpensive
- distribution of the CD. Frequently the hardest stage in the process, distribution is the process of (a) persuading shops to stock the record, then (b) ensuring that the stock is delivered on time and in the right quantities.

If all the stages have been managed properly, then it's just a matter of letting the shops' customers buy the record! Of course, it's never that simple. CD sales are very volatile. Record companies need to make profits from consistently successful recording artists in order to cover losses made elsewhere – another necessary risk in the business of popular music. Every year many artists are signed by record companies but their records are unsuccessful and they fail to repay the companies' investment. Also, as musical fashions change or as artists' inspiration runs out, last year's big seller can easily become this year's loss.

Majors and independents

This distinction between companies is widely used in the record industry. Generally speaking, international companies which own their own **distribution** networks worldwide (see the list at the very top of page 14) are referred to as 'majors', whereas 'independent' labels produce records that are then supplied to other companies for distribution. Needless to say, there are grey areas. Major companies will often invest in apparently independent labels and there are also independents who handle a certain amount of distribution.

Popular music and radio

Radio has been one of the most important media in the development of popular music this century.

The beginnings of radio

Since its first development as an entertainment medium in the 1920s and '30s, radio has been a very important 'primary source' for listeners to popular music. Often people would not be able to travel to live performances, and recordings and the equipment to play them on were still relatively expensive. However, as of late 1922, anyone could buy a radio and, by paying an annual licence fee of ten shillings (50p), listen to the rather worthy mixture of news, speeches, lectures, educational programmes, weather reports and, almost as an afterthought, drama and music, which was broadcast at the time. Music seemed to be regarded as being of relatively little importance for such a

significant new medium, which, interestingly, had also been the case when sound recording was invented! Sir John (later Lord) Reith, the first Director General of the BBC, regarded the popular dance music of the time as trivial and unworthy of airtime.

Broadcasts of concerts became a feature of radio stations in the USA during this time, partly because the crackling, hissing surface noise of shellac **78 rpm** records was deemed too obtrusive. However, by the 1930s and '40s the radio and recording industries were constantly in dispute about the playing of recordings 'on air'. Listeners would also have strong views about the two media, with record buyers generally disapproving of the down-market appeal of 'the wireless'.

Radio Luxembourg

'Because we all drink Ovaltine,
   we're happy girls and boys!'

This was just one of the advertising **jingles** featured on Radio Luxembourg, the first station to challenge the BBC for UK popular music radio audiences.

Published in 1983, the cover of this book conveys a perfect impression of its era. Interestingly, another publication connected with Radio Luxembourg – a magazine called 'Fab 208' after the station's medium wave frequency (announced on-air with the jingle 'Fabulous two-oh-eight!') – was an early example of cross-media image exploitation.

The charts

This situation was to change when the link between the broadcasting of records and 'the charts' became established in the 1950s. It then became clear that the broadcasting of records could have a direct and dramatic effect on sales. The crude but logical technique of ranking recordings in order of popularity was particularly effective; and so the charts were born.

Radio rivalry

In the UK, the new broadcasting industry was dominated by the BBC, which was funded by radio licence fees and a 10% **royalty** on all radio sets sold.

This monopoly was first threatened by the launch of Radio Luxembourg in 1933. The station broadcast a mixture of news, music and entertainment in its early days. Funded by advertising and American-style programme sponsorship (which resulted in popular artists of the day being featured in such items as *The Kraft Cheese Concert*), the station evolved over the following decades into a popular music phenomenon. Its lively style was aimed at winning listeners from the more staid BBC Light Programme (now Radio 2), the Home Service (now Radio 4) and the classical Third Programme (now Radio 3).

In the 1960s, the first wave of pirate radio stations presented the strongest challenge yet to the BBC's position, accelerating the development of popular music radio. Typically operating from ships anchored just outside British waters, most notable among these were Radio London and Radio Caroline.

When legislation finally closed down these pirate stations in 1967, the BBC decided to capture the now-abandoned audiences for popular music with a shake-up of its radio stations, launching a brand new service, BBC Radio 1. Staffed almost entirely by DJs who

had worked for the pirates, this was the first official UK radio station devoted to modern pop music.

Pop radio today

Today, the popular music output of BBC national radio is supplemented by a range of alternative stations, including both BBC regional stations and independents. Some, such as Jazz FM and Capital Gold, specialize in particular genres of popular music. Also, the compact nature and reduced cost of modern broadcasting technology has allowed a new wave of pirate stations to appear, as well as short-term licensed stations which are often linked to particular events such as festivals. However, one thing has not changed, and that is the importance of radio airplay to popular music.

Radio romantics

For many years, popular musicians have paid tribute to the importance of radio in their songs, acknowledging the significance of the medium in their chosen career. Here are two examples:

You had the time, you had the power, you've yet to have your finest hour, radio! Queen, 'Radio Ga Ga', 1984

Cruisin' and playin' the radio, with no particular place to go. Chuck Berry, 'No Particular Place to Go', 1964

There are probably many more examples, and a second generation of acknowledgements is now beginning to arise. For example, the well-known contemporary rock band Radiohead named themselves after the David Byrne/Talking Heads song of that name.

Popular music and television

The importance of television to popular music is a paradox. How does modern popular music fit into a family entertainment medium?

Virtually since its first widespread use in public broadcasting in the 1950s, television has tended to occupy the place once held by radio as a source of family entertainment.

As radios became smaller, lighter and cheaper (some radio now fit into the user's ear), televisions became more sophisticated. However, a large visual image is equated with quality, excitement and viewing comfort. While the availability of small portable televisions did change the TV into a product which can be duplicated in a single household (and TV receiver cards for personal computers are now also available), the advent of stereo TV sound broadcasting and video, together with 'home cinema' TV set-ups, has emphasized sound quality, with greater implications for music broadcasting.

Pop on TV

Popular music has always relied on the contrasting tastes of succeeding generations of listeners to sustain its creativity. Malcolm McLaren, producer and one-time manager of controversial bands like the Sex Pistols, stated that the role of popular music was to create generation gaps. This of course contradicts the cross-generational power of television as a medium. When, during the heyday of punk in the 1970s, the Sex Pistols obligingly swore on

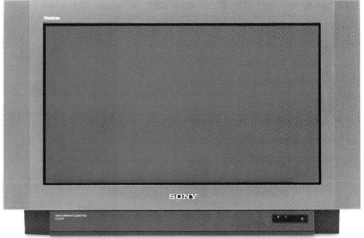

The availability of 'hi-fi' TV sound has important implications for popular music on TV and video.

the chat show hosted by Bill Grundy (at Grundy's prompting), the situation not only showed up this contradiction but, naturally, caused an uproar among the pre-punk generation of viewers.

Despite this, chart and panel shows devoted to popular music have had a strong presence in the medium of television for many years. These have recently been augmented by some highly successful documentaries (often called 'rockumentaries') covering individual artists, bands and genres. Add to this the use of popular music in non-music programmes (popular musicians appear on shows ranging from *Blue Peter* to daytime chat shows), and as theme or background music for drama shows, and it becomes clear that popular music and television are closely interconnected.

Pop in advertising

The use of music in TV commercials is now quite a complex subject. Originally used either to provide a pleasant background noise for a spoken **voice-over**, or in the form of a song about the product, music is now chosen carefully to fit the target market for the product, according to age and lifestyle. Ironically, it is often impossible to obtain permission to use artists' original recordings for this purpose, which means that **session musicians** are used to create very close copies of the original tunes.

I want my MTV!

Since the 1980s, the widespread enthusiasm for popular music videos has had a dramatic impact on popular music on television. MTV (Music Television) is a cable channel which was started in the USA in 1981, broadcasting continuous popular music videos, the production costs of which are funded by the artists' record companies. By the end of the decade it had become very popular both with the younger end of the pop market but also

with young adult listeners. By 1991 the channel had 28 million subscribers and was adding between one and three million new subscribers every year, reaching 85% of 18–34 year-olds in the USA.

The European subsidiary, MTV Europe, was launched in 1988. Broadcasting 24 hours a day, MTV Europe now reaches 44 million homes. MTV Asia, launched in 1991, covers more than 30 countries from the Middle East to Japan.

That's the way you do it!

Some artists have expressed reservations about the aggressive commercialism of the MTV empire, implying that the channel's wide audience is a product of an unadventurous, market-led approach which is governed entirely by fashion. However, the massive penetration of MTV into popular culture has undoubtedly attracted the attention of audiences who would otherwise be less likely to follow popular music.

The lyrics of the 1995 song 'Money for Nothing', written by Mark Knopfler, guitarist, singer and songwriter of the British rock band Dire Straits, are supposedly based on a conversation between two American domestic appliance fitters overheard in a bar. The song describes how playing a guitar on MTV is not a real job, and how the performer can enjoy a luxurious, hedonistic lifestyle in return for very little effort.

The intention is scathingly satirical, with the implication being that this kind of listener is entirely cynical about successful rock bands and believes a conventional job to be much more hard work than being a musician.

Popular music and video

The rise of video has added a new dimension to popular music, but has at the same time failed to deliver the revolution some artists were hoping for.

Video first became a routine part of popular music in the 1970s, when the technology necessary to record and replay the medium became affordable to both producers and consumers of popular music.

The format fairly quickly assumed two roles:
• a promotional tool for TV stations and for viewing primarily by the industry
• a consumer medium, both as a take-home purchase, available from record shops, and as a broadcast product.

Before video

Prior to the widespread use of consumer video, the effort that many artists (together with their designers and producers) put into the visual aspect of their performance was often fleeting in its impact, at least in terms of action.

Stage shows, however elaborate, could often only be referred to with still photography, album cover art or occasionally film, which

Bismillah, no! The first rock vid-e-o!

At the height of glam-rock in 1975, when lurid make-up and glitter was deemed to be the way forward for rock music, the band Queen produced what is generally regarded as the forerunner of the dramatic popular music videos which are commonplace today.

The single 'Bohemian Rhapsody' condensed a large, near-operatic story-line into one side of a single. The accompanying visuals were equally audacious and drew on as much camera trickery as possible to add to the whole over-the-top imagery of the song. The special effects seem quaintly primitive today. The song achieved a new notoriety when mimed along to during a car journey by the protagonists in the film *Wayne's World*.

*This is how the **overdubbed** voices of a mock 'opera chorus' in Queen's single 'Bohemian Rhapsody' were represented visually.*

would often be made under unsuitable conditions. Films on popular music subjects would generally be devised as cinema feature presentations, with at least a pretence to a plot within which the artists' talents could be showcased (such as the numerous films starring the Beatles, Elvis Presley and Cliff Richard) or as straightforward concert footage (such as the festival film *Woodstock*). Television appearances, being confined to an ordinary TV studio, would generally be very contained affairs, in which the artists would simply play (or mime) their latest hits.

Cut to the present day

The **editing**, special effects and production values offered by video were to change all this. Not only could the visual aspect of the artist's performance be highlighted in a continuous, repeatable experience, but the whole concept could be presented in a stylish and imaginative way, with perfect production values achievable both visually and in terms of the music. This means that artists are now able to produce videos that are as sophisticated as any cinema presentation. For example, the video that accompanied Michael Jackson's 1982 album *Thriller*, directed by the renowned film director John Landis, used astonishing special effects, which no doubt helped the album's sales of some 47 million copies.

Because the ideas in music videos must be highly condensed – in the case of a video associated with a single release, often down to a very few minutes – the style of many pop videos is often a remarkable exercise in rapid-fire imagery.

Fifteen years ago, the singer Adam Ant wrote: 'I'm sure the public will be swift to adopt the video disc and remarks like "Have you seen and heard so-and-so's new single?" [will] become commonplace.' Although this prediction has proved to be inaccurate, new developments such as the DVD – a CD-sized video disc – will offer new possibilities.

I'm single, bilingual ...

One of the best pop videos of more recent years accompanied the single 'Bilingual' by the Pet Shop Boys. The **lyrics** are a gentle send-up of young Euro-businesspeople. The video contains a witty selection of images, including some very energetic dancing by a grey-suited group of 'yuppies' of both sexes.

The video promoting the CD *Bilingual* by the Pet Shop Boys contains lots of memorable imagery – unlike the quietly cool CD cover.

The video also incorporates several references to the arms trade, which perhaps provides many of the business people depicted with their livelihoods! These references include fighter planes and a rather military-sounding corps of drums. This also shows an interesting example of the contrasts between video and televisual presentation of popular music. When the band performed this single on BBC TV's *Top of the Pops*, in the full glare of the studio lighting, great care was taken to place the most attractive looking members of the drum corps at the front of the group!

Popular music and film

These two art forms have been linked ever since the first 'talkie'. Today, popular music and film intermingle in a bewildering variety of ways.

Where it all began

The very first full-length film with a recorded soundtrack had a popular music subject and featured a widely acclaimed singer. Al Jolson, an American singer and actor, was able to combine both talents in a film presentation for the very first time in *The Jazz Singer*, released in 1927.

The (white!) American performer Al Jolson was noted for his 'blacked-up' performances, drawn from the American minstrel tradition. Respect for African-American culture was not high on the social agenda of the period.

From Sinatra to Spice

Ever since then, popular music and films have enjoyed a mutually supportive relationship, which seems to have explored every permutation of music, dance, song, biography, fiction and narrative. A few examples:
• Frank Sinatra was a key performer in stage musicals interpreted on film. This has been a popular form for many years. Key film musicals include *The Wizard of Oz* (1939), *On the Town* (1949, starring Sinatra), *West Side Story* (1957), *The Sound of Music* (1959) and *Jesus Christ Superstar* (1970).
• Most Indian films include musical interludes, regardless of their theme.
• David Bowie capitalized on his otherworldly image created during his musical career when he was cast as an alien in *The Man Who Fell to Earth* (1976).
• The Beatles made several successful films with a strong musical element, including *A Hard Day's Night* (1964) and *Help* (1968).
• Elvis Presley's popularity was enhanced by his many films, including *GI Blues* (1960) and *Blue Hawaii* (1961).
• Concerts such as *Pink Floyd at Pompeii* (1972) were filmed for cinema release.
• The Spice Girls recently starred in a tenuously plotted musical adventure, *Spiceworld* (1997).

SPICEWORLD

THE MOVIE

With Spiceworld, *the Spice Girls were continuing a 70-year-old tradition of popular music stars making films.*

Inextricably linked

Since the 1980s, the links between popular music and film have become much more complex. As several generations have now grown up with both the modern popular music tradition and the high-profile film-making industry, the imagery of the two has become mingled in the consciousness of both producers and consumers. Examples of this heightened interaction include:

• an increasing number of popular music 'biopics' – biographical films presented as drama. These have included studies of the lead singer of the Doors, Jim Morrison (*The Doors*, 1991), and the brutalized early life of Tina

Turner (*What's Love Got To Do With It?*, 1993)

• the explicit linking of the two cultures by naming films after popular songs, seemingly just to capitalize on the association these titles have for the films' target audiences. This provides another way in which the audience can relate to the film and is similar to the use of 'classic' pop songs in TV commercials (see page 19). These films have included song titles spanning most of this century, including *Paper Moon* (1973), *Radio On* (1979) and *Stand By Me* (1986)

• the rise of film music as a recognized art form.

Music, image and irony

There are some memorable instances where a film draws attention through internal reference to some of the 'trickery' used in popular music and recording technology. Film, of course, is even more dependent than music on editing, effects and general interference with the 'natural' approach to performance!

In the science fiction film Battlestar Galactica, *one of the lead characters encounters a group of alien singers each of whom has two voices (and two mouths!), which they can sing with simultaneously, thus doubling the number of voices in the group. This is one possible solution to the problem of how to produce overdubbed voices live!*

In the allegorical film Gattaca, *human beings are genetically engineered to achieve perfection. One result of this is a pianist with six fingers on each hand. In the film the pianist plays a piece by the classical composer Schubert which has had extra notes subtly added to it to show the effect this would have. No need to use* **sequencers** *on stage any more to help out with those tricky keyboard parts!*

Popular music and the press

Music criticism is probably as old as music itself.

Coverage of popular music in the press is very substantial. It includes:

• the national newspapers – which often have a regular column devoted to popular music as occasional feature articles

• the music press – which now covers every area of musical taste and every **demographic group**

• 'lifestyle' magazines for men and women, such as *GQ* and *Elle* – which often include an element of music coverage

• fanzines – amateur magazines produced by fans of a particular artist, band or type of music

• poster magazines – mainly consisting of large-scale visuals of particular artists

• musicians' magazines – which are mainly targeted at performers and recording artists at all levels, although serious amateur musicians and semi-professional players (who make some money through music but also have another occupation) will make up a large percentage of the readers.

The wide variety of music magazines has been made possible because there are now so many different kinds of popular music, each with its own group of listeners. Also, modern desktop publishing technology makes it very easy to design and produce magazines.

Reading music

Here are some diverse examples from the music press:

• *Q* is a long-established general popular music monthly

• *Mixmag* is devoted almost exclusively to dance music

• *Kerrang!* deals exclusively with heavy metal

• *The Source* covers the diverse popular music created by black artists

• *Rhythm* serves a subset (drummers) of a subset (musicians) of the overall following for popular music.

• *NME* is a weekly music magazine which has survived for several decades.

• The national press also covers popular music, like this TV Guide.

Contents

A typical music magazine may include:
• features on one or more artists, discussing their work in reasonable depth and possibly based on interview material
• 'think pieces' – feature-length material offering a more theoretical critical approach
• reviews of recordings and/or events
• news items, including advance notification of events.

Cross-media promotion

The magazine format is a very adaptable product in terms of where it can be sold. Music magazines are available in record stores, newsagents, at special events and via postal subscription. This has led to many types of cross-media promotion and instances of magazines working together with other music industry organizations. These include cover-mounted CDs, which today are almost a necessary part of a music magazine (some titles carry them every month). Such CDs tend to be 'samplers' – a range of material licensed from record companies, covering a period of time or a type of music.

Sponsorship and influence

Music magazines are now as much a part of the popular music scene as the music itself. This high profile is often put to good use, such as when a magazine sponsors a festival. There are also more controversial examples. The weekly *NME* (*New Musical Express*) was once accused of over-inflating the musical success of the 'Madchester' scene – the rock and dance culture centred on Manchester – purely to contrive a sense of exclusivity, thereby boosting the magazine's circulation in a cynical way.

Here to stay?

Despite new sources of news and comment such as the Internet, expertly written specialist magazines on all subjects, including music, are probably here to stay and will continue to improve and diversify. After all, they are cheap, widely available, convenient, pleasing to read and require no specialist knowledge or equipment other than the ability to read and enough light to read by!

Natalie Imbruglia at the Q *awards – a typical example of a popular music magazine sponsoring an event.*

'Can we bleed this into the gutter?'

(This means: 'Can we run this advertisement on two facing pages, with the image joined together on the edge where the two pages are bound in?')

Commercial music magazines depend on advertising for a lot of their regular revenue, much of which comes from record companies. The influence of the music press is now so strong that advertising is often placed to attract the attention of record retailers as much as the public. The dealers will use the music press as a guide to what should be in stock in their shops.

Popular music and the new media

The production and consumption of popular music has now colonized a whole range of new media, including computer **software**, the Internet and new **digital** audio media.

For most of this century, there have really been only three ways in which people could interact with popular music. They could either perform it live themselves, listen to someone else performing it live, or hear it 'canned' on either a recording, a radio or television broadcast or in a film.

Over the past thirty years, however, two factors have allowed popular music to expand in many other directions: the arrival of affordable digital media and the blurring of the distinctions between recorded music, live music, listening and performance.

Digital

Digital techniques allow sound to be stored as computer data. This essentially means that every aspect of the music – pitch, timbre, rhythm and so on – can be stored and transmitted as a series of electronic ones and zeroes. Digital technology can assemble and reproduce this data at astonishing speed. Thanks to this speed, all the information

Consuming or producing?

This is one of the various varieties of software called Koan produced by the British company SSEYO. Koan enables the user to mix a wide variety of supplied sounds, short melodies, chords, rhythms and effects to produce original music, using just an ordinary computer. The graphics represent each sound as an icon, which is placed onto a background. The sound will be higher or lower and come more from the left or the right, depending on where it is placed on the background. The sounds

will continue to repeat, each at their own pace, unless they are changed. The sounds can also be made to change their loudness and position at random. This means that once the user has set up the piece of music, it will go on changing as it plays, producing different results each time.

This is a new kind of popular music, which is neither completely composed by the software user, nor bought 'ready-to-listen-to' like a conventional audio CD.

needed to reproduce music can be stored, transmitted and replayed very easily.

The most obvious and widespread development of this technology has been the compact disc, which was originally marketed as a replacement for the vinyl record. However, as the CD format is also used for multimedia computer data (**CD-ROM**), many innovative variations were to follow. These include:

• interactive CD-ROM music releases, such as Peter Gabriel's *XPLORA 1*. This was the first widely available release that not only included music but also allowed PC users to remix a selection of Gabriel's music and have an onscreen 'virtual tour' of his studio

• 'multi-session' and 'mixed-mode' CDs, which are able to carry both music (in the standard format for playing on an ordinary CD player) and CD-ROM data. This means that the user can play the disc to hear the music in the usual way but also use the CD in a computer to access the software, which is usually related to the music in some way. CDs that are cover-mounted on magazines are often in mixed-mode format. The software can take the form of a multimedia record catalogue, short video interviews with musicians, composition programmes and so on

• interactive composition software, such as Mixman Studio and Koan. Compositional software, which enables musicians to create and **sequence** sounds using a computer, has existed for many years. More recently, however, many CD-ROMs have been produced which allow the user to assemble and mix pieces of music from a selection of 'pre-composed' elements – half-way between creating and listening to popular music

The Net

The Internet (Net or World Wide Web) has also provided popular music with an entirely

new area in which to operate. As it is now relatively easy and inexpensive to set up a Web site on the Internet – allowing computer users all over the world to call up both sound and visual information – popular music has a very widespread and diverse presence on the 'information superhighway'. Just a few examples include:

• Internet 'radio stations', which transmit music, interviews with musicians, and so on across the Internet to anyone who wishes to access the site. For example: Capital FM at http://www.capitalfm.co.uk

• 'fan pages', in which followers of particular artists share information about, and photographs of, their favourite performers. For example: http://www.geocities.com/ Hollywood/ Academy/2425/kyliemain.html is a fan site devoted to the singer Kylie Minogue.

Kylie Minogue Page

Here's what you can do on the page:

Pictures
News
Links

Last updated: 23rd July 1997

This Internet site is typical of many set up by fans to support their favourite artists. This site features Kylie Minogue. One effect of the ease with which Web sites can be set up is that supporters of popular music that is either no longer fashionable, or which has yet to become fashionable, or which is unlikely ever to be truly fashionable, are still able to share information and news without the need for commercial media, such as the music press.

Media cross-currents

Music, being less dependent on language than literature or drama, has always tended to transcend national boundaries. Now, more than ever before, popular music is transcending media boundaries with equal ease.

Much of this book has dealt with media other than the media which are usually associated with music, such as recordings and radio. Popular music has in fact always worked its way into new media, in many cases since their very beginnings. This is perhaps mainly due to popular music's ability to bypass language barriers while at the same time reflect universal experiences.

Media cross-overs

Popular music has become a phenomenon shared all over the world. This has happened because of the ever-expanding world market for musical styles derived from the UK and the USA, and also by mixing in musical influences from non-Western countries. Having crossed the world's national boundaries, popular music is now crossing the barriers between conventional media. Some recent examples include:

• music magazines on videocassette
• CDs appearing as audio supplements to books about popular music
• record catalogues on **CD-ROM**, together with audio examples
• a constant redefining of the experience of popular music, such as its use on television commercials.

Back to its roots

Popular music is often at its most ingenious when it steps back from its conventional media role. Recording technology, which was originally expected to be used mainly for spoken word recordings, has finally returned to these roots with the availability of interview discs, which often have no music at all.

Music and soup

This recording also manages to be an advertising vehicle for Heinz soup! Conversely, the Heinz TV commercial featuring the music of this group has provided national advertising for the group's sound, thus allowing cross-media advertising for both products.

Flaunting it

Sigue Sigue Sputnik was a rock band formed in the UK in the mid-1980s. Unlike artist-driven bands, 'Sputnik' was deliberately created with a view to achieving success through media attention. For example, the band's outrageous appearance ensured that they had considerable press coverage, including in the disapproving tabloid newspapers, before they had even released any records.

This technique was not new. The Sex Pistols and the Monkees were among many bands that had also been created to exploit the connections between popular music and the media. However, Sigue Sigue Sputnik carried the process a stage further by including advertisements, similar to radio advertisements, between the tracks of the band's debut album *Flaunt It*.

Media diversity

Today, a single piece of popular music could theoretically appear in any of the following forms:

- CD
- cassette
- vinyl version for DJ use
- video
- TV special
- official souvenir book
- unofficial souvenir book
- transcription of part of the music in a musicians' magazine
- karaoke tape
- **MIDI** file for playback through a computer or **sequencer**
- Web site
- PC game …
… and much more.

This indicates that popular music's ability to be part of all available media has expanded as new media have become available.

Big business

Popular music itself is more diverse now than at any other time in its history, and this is reflected in the wide range of media available to the form. Of course, like all areas of modern popular culture, popular music has grown up in a market-led society. This means that, as a large-scale industry, the music will continue to be controlled by corporate 'patrons', who will make money, loose money, buy each other's companies and generally behave as businesses do. However, there can be no successful business without talent – and talent remains central to popular music.

Timeline

Pop music: a pretty ancient idea ...

First century BC	Roman and Alexandrine entertainers travel from town to town performing popular music.
1100-1500	Travelling minstrels and troubadours perform popular music in Europe.
1728	First performance of *The Beggar's Opera* by John Gay, which combined popular song forms with structured presentation. The work is a great success.
1781	America achieves independence.
1864	First modern professional songwriter, the American Stephen Foster, dies aged 38.
1877	Thomas Edison invents the phonograph, which can record sound on to wax cylinders.
1890s	US music publishing industry produces vast numbers of popular songs in sheet music form.
1895	First mass-produced **78 rpm** records go on sale.
1920s	Nearly 100 million records manufactured each year in the USA alone.
1931	First electric guitar introduced by the American company Rickenbacker, nicknamed 'the frying pan' because of its shape.
1935	Big band swing – an upbeat, rhythmic form derived from jazz – becomes the most popular musical form.
1939	World War II begins.
1945	With the end of World War II, interest in individual pop singers surpasses that of bands.
1948	LP (long playing) records introduced, allowing around 40 minutes of music to appear on one disc.
1954	Bill Haley releases 'Rock Around the Clock' – one of the earliest rock 'n' roll records.
1964	The Beatles perform in New York – the British influence on modern pop music worldwide begins.
1970s	Diverse types of pop music, such as disco, glam, punk, new wave, reggae and funk – are all recognized as different kinds of music with their own followings.
1983	Launch of compact disc (CD).
1990s	Pop music mixes more influences than ever before, including non-western music and revivals of earlier styles.

... that's still around!

Maybe we should wait for the Roman and Alexandrine revival!

Glossary

amplification making sounds louder by using electrical devices (e.g. microphone, amplifier and loudspeakers)

CD-ROM stands for Compact Disc Read-Only Memory, which is a compact disc with software (for text, sounds and/or graphics) that can be played on a computer but which cannot be altered or added to by the user

censored adjective describing texts or pictures that have been changed, either by a government or other authority, because their content is believed to be offensive, dangerous or illegal

demographic group term used by researchers to describe a section of the population with similarities of age, background and lifestyle (e.g. 'educated professional men aged 25–40 who buy ten or more CDs per year')

digital information stored electronically as a sequence of ones and zeros

distribution process of bringing recordings (or any other goods) from the companies that make them to the shops that sell them. It includes transportation, warehousing, order processing.

double-tracking repeat recording of someone singing or playing 'on top of' (or 'behind') a track they have recorded previously – see also **overdubbing**

editing making changes to a film, text or piece of music after it is first produced in order to improve it still further in preparation for final large-scale production

jingle short, easily recognizable piece of music used in advertising or to signal a particular part, such as a traffic report, in a radio programme

lyrics words in a song, **jingle**, etc.

merchandising products such as T-shirts, posters and souvenirs which depict pop artists and are bought by fans to show their support; merchandising is also used in other media, such as film and television

MIDI stands for musical Instrument Digital Interface, and enables computers, synthesizers and **sequencers** to 'talk' to each other, using agreed standards for hardware and **software**. MIDI sound files are easy to modify and manipulate

overdubbing adding additional musical parts to a recording, on top of other parts – see also **double-tracking**

PA stands for 'Public Address' system – the equipment used in pop and rock concerts through which the sound from the various microphones is **amplified**

royalty fee paid to an inventor, writer or composer in proportion to the number of products sold containing or using their ideas or material

sell-through process that describes the marketing and selling of a product on the strength of the popularity of an earlier, related product (e.g. selling a single, an album containing the single, and a video relating to the album – all by the same artist)

sequenced adjective describing music that has been stored, recorded or played with a **digital sequencer**. A sequencer can be in the form of an instrument with a digital memory designed for this purpose, or a piece **software** that runs on an ordinary computer

session musicians musicians who are hired to play on individual recordings but who are not regular members of the band; the term is also sometimes used to describe musicians with the same role when a band or artist performs live

78 rpm 78 revolutions per minute – the speed of rotation of early records

software computer data which instructs the computer to perform certain tasks, such as memorizing musical notes (or the text of this book!)

voice-over spoken commentary added to music or some other background sound

Index